DINOSAUR DAYS

VELOCIRAPTOR
The Swift Hunter

Benchmark Books
Marshall Cavendish Corporation
99 White Plains Road
Tarrytown, New York 10591-9001

Scientific consultant:
Rolf Johnson, Associate Curator of Paleontology;
Director, Science Media Center; Milwaukee Public Museum

Library of Congress Cataloging-in-Publication
Riehecky, Janet, date.
Velociraptor : the swift hunter / Janet Riehecky ;
p.   cm -- (Dinosaur days)
Includes bibliographical references (p. -) and index.
Summary: Describes the lives of the small, but ferocious dinosaurs
that became widely known after being featured
in the movie, "Jurassic Park."
ISBN 0-7614-0603-4
1. Velociraptor--Juvenile literature. [1. Velociraptor. 2. Dinosaurs.]
I. Title. II. Series: Riehecky, Janet, date. Dinosaur Days.
QE862.S3R55   1998   567.912--dc21   96-48743   CIP   AC

Printed in the United States of America

1 3 5 7 8 6 4 2

DINOSAUR DAYS

VELOCIRAPTOR
The Swift Hunter

WRITTEN BY JANET RIEHECKY
ILLUSTRATED BY SUSAN TOLONEN

BENCHMARK BOOKS

MARSHALL CAVENDISH
NEW YORK

Velociraptor slept in the shade of a tall cliff. Around her slept four other Velociraptors, the members of her pack. As the morning sun began to lighten the sky, she awoke. Velociraptor scratched at an insect bite, then stretched. It was going to be hot that day, but then most of the days were hot.

The other members of the pack also began to stir. They stood and stretched, sniffing one another and walking about. Each watched the first Velociraptor, their leader, for direction. They were all eager to begin the day. They had not caught any food the day before, and they were hungry.

Velociraptor stared out across the land. As far as she could see there was nothing but sand—mound after mound of sand piled into gently rolling hills. It looked empty, but *Velociraptor* knew it wasn't. Out there somewhere there was food. So off she went, heading out across the sand dunes. She didn't look back to see if her pack followed. She knew they would.

Velociraptor and her pack left two-toed footprints in the sand, but the prints didn't last very long. The wind blew, and within minutes sand had filled them. Soon there was no sign that anything had ever walked that way.

Every now and then, *Velociraptor* stopped. First she tilted her head and listened. Then she sniffed the air, looked to the right and then quickly to the left. Her stomach grumbled, but each time there was no prey nearby. Her pack trailed after her, moving silently.

Once, *Velociraptor* saw something move on the side of a sand dune. A lizard scurried past. *Velociraptor* moved quickly, snapping at it with her sharp teeth. She was fast, but the lizard was faster. She missed, and the creature got away.

8

The pack moved across the sand dunes. In the distance
Velociraptor could see a pair of *Pinacosaurs*, armored dinosaurs.
She watched them for a moment, then turned the other way.
No dinner there. The only soft spot on them was their bellies.
The rest of those creatures was covered with bony armor. Little
Pinacosaurs could be flipped over on their backs, but these two
were too big.

As they traveled on, *Velociraptor* stumbled across a dead *Oviraptor*. She and the pack sniffed at its bones, but a scavenger had already eaten everything that could be eaten. No dinner there.

Velociraptor didn't worry. She could smell water. Where there was water, there were plants. And where there were plants, there were plant eaters.

Near the top of the next sand dune *Velociraptor* stopped. She chose a spot where the wind would blow the scent of her pack away from any prey. Then she peered over the top. She saw a herd of *Protoceratops* at an oasis beyond the dune. Dinner!

Velociraptor and her pack studied the scene. A spring had formed a fairly large pond, an oasis in the desert. She could see turtles and several large crocodiles in its waters. Near its edge grew small shrubs, flowers, and a few trees. But the best part was that there were about thirty *Protoceratops* chewing on the plants in and by the oasis. None of them seemed aware that there were meat eaters nearby.

Velociraptor examined the herd. She wanted to find an animal that had wandered away from the main body of the herd. It would help if the animal was hurt already or was very young or very old. Those animals would have a hard time defending themselves.

Soon she saw what she needed. An older *Protoceratops* started pulling away from the herd. He was headed for some bushes at the edge of the oasis. He was bigger than *Velociraptor*, but not by much. And he was limping just a bit.

Once *Velociraptor* decided, she moved quickly. She dashed across the sand dune, trying to get between the *Protoceratops* and his herd. Her pack followed close behind.

As *Velociraptor* raced across the sand, the *Protoceratops* herd began bellowing in alarm. Some of them ran off into the desert, but most of them gathered together facing toward the pack. By working together, they could defend themselves against most meat eaters.

But *Velociraptor* wasn't interested in the herd. She kept her eyes on the older *Protoceratops* she had selected. He was trying to get to the herd, but she and her pack were too fast for him. They ran between him and the herd and forced him to move farther away.

Protoceratops turned one direction, then another. There was no place to go. The pack had him surrounded. He knew he couldn't run away, so he turned to fight.

For just a moment, the two looked at each other. Then *Velociraptor* leaped toward *Protoceratops*. The huge claws on her feet came slashing down. The *Protoceratops* tried to bite *Velociraptor* with his strong beak, but *Velociraptor* quickly dodged away. She grasped *Protoceratops* by the frill covering his neck and shoulders and slashed again into his belly. The pack members slashed at his side. *Protoceratops* had lost. The pack had its food.

After eating their fill, the pack wandered over to the pond to drink some water. The *Protoceratops* herd had run away, but there was still lots of life at the oasis. Insects buzzed, and turtles played in the water. One crocodile stayed, but he swam to the far side of the pond. He might be able to beat *Velociraptor* in a fight, but he might not. And he didn't really want to know which it would be.

The pack took a long nap in the cool of the oasis. Then they headed out across the dunes.

The pack had not been traveling again for long when, suddenly, the wind shifted. A huge, dark cloud appeared in the distance. It began rolling toward the pack, growing bigger and bigger until it seemed to fill all the sky. The sand began to swirl around and lift into the air. The pack huddled together. They knew this meant danger. It was a sandstorm!

The sands whirled around, battering at the pack. It stung their skin and made it hard to breathe. There was nothing that they could do, except snuggle together and wait for it to stop.

Finally the winds slowed and then stopped. Several inches of sand covered the pack of *Velociraptors*, but they stood up and shook it off. No one in the pack seemed to be badly hurt. They stretched, then sniffed each other to be sure everyone was all right. Then the pack moved on.

    Velociraptor led her pack into a winding canyon, seeking a good place to spend the night. It had been a long day. As the sun began to set, she found just the right spot—a small opening in the side of a cliff that would provide protection and comfort.

    Velociraptor settled down next to the cliff. Then she and her pack closed their eyes and drifted into sleep.

SOME FACTS ABOUT . . . VELOCIRAPTOR

Physical Appearance

Velociraptor became famous twice. In 1971 in Mongolia, scientists found fossil bones of a *Velociraptor* and a *Protoceratops* together. The *Protoceratops* had the arm of the *Velociraptor* in its mouth. The *Velociraptor* was holding onto the *Protoceratops*'s frill with its hands and had the huge claws on its feet in the *Protoceratops*'s stomach. Apparently, they both died at the same time. Either they each killed the other, or both were killed by some force of nature, such as a sandstorm. There were many stories in the papers and on television about these "fighting dinosaurs." Scientists were excited about the fossils. Most of the time, scientists have to imagine how the dinosaurs lived. They look at teeth and claws and other clues and try to figure out what the dinosaurs did. They also look at how similar animals that are alive today act. The actions of the *Velociraptors* in this story were figured out that way. But scientists don't have to guess with the fighting dinosaurs. They can see how *Velociraptor* attacked its prey and how *Protoceratops* defended itself.

Velociraptor became famous again in 1994 in a movie called *Jurassic Park*. But the *Velociraptors* shown in that movie were not quite accurate. *Velociraptor* was actually a small meat eater, just about six feet (1.8 meters) long and standing only about as tall as a man's chest. The producers made the movie dinosaur bigger to be more dramatic. The skull of *Velociraptor* is also longer and flatter than the one shown in the movie. The movie dinosaur was actually more like *Deinonychus*, a relative of *Velociraptor*.

The Swift Hunter

Velociraptor might have been small, but the movie *Jurassic Park* was right about its being a ferocious hunter. It had very sharp teeth and strong arms, with sharp claws on all its fingers. And it also had a very special claw on each foot. *Velociraptors* have four toes on their feet. The first toe, on the inside part of the foot, is very small. The third and fourth toes are large and have very small claws. But the second toe has a huge claw that could move up and down, somewhat like a switchblade. *Velociraptor* could walk on just the third and fourth toes, with the huge claw lifted up, so it would stay sharp. Scientists also think

Velociraptor could run very fast to chase its prey. Few animals could have defended themselves against such a creature.

Velociraptors were certainly fierce hunters, but they did not kill because they were mean. They killed only for food. They had to eat meat to stay alive.

In fact, these fierce hunters may have been very loving parents. A relative of *Velociraptor* named *Oviraptor* was. Scientists found the bones of an *Oviraptor* on top of a nest of fossil eggs. It was clear that that dinosaur was sitting on the eggs, protecting them, when it died. Scientists think *Oviraptors* took very good care of their babies after they hatched, too. *Velociraptors* might have done the same thing.

GLOSSARY

frill . . . . a large, bony plate that covered the neck and shoulders of some dinosaurs

oasis . . . . an area in a desert where there is water and plants can grow

pack . . . . a group of animals, usually meat eaters, that live together

prey . . . . an animal that is hunted and killed for food

sand dune . . . . a large mound of sand, often as tall as a hill

scavenger . . . . a creature that finds animals that are already dead to eat

scent . . . . smell

switchblade . . . . . . a pocketknife with a spring-operated blade that opens instantly when a release on the handle is pressed

FOR FURTHER READING

Bakker, Robert T. *Raptor Red.* Thorndike, ME: Thorndike Press, 1995.

Cole, Joanna. *The Magic School Bus in the Time of the Dinosaurs.* New York: Scholastic, 1994.

Dixon, Dougal. *Dinosaurs: A Closer Look.* Jackson, TN: Davidson Titles, Inc., 1994.

Dixon, Dougal. *Dougal Dixon's Dinosaurs.* Honesdale, PA: Boyds Mills Press, 1993.

Farlow, James Orville. *On the Tracks of Dinosaurs.* New York: Franklin Watts, 1991.

Novacek, Michael. *Dinosaurs of the Flaming Cliffs.* New York: Doubleday, 1996.

Parker, Steve. *Dinosaurs and How They Lived.* New York: Dorling Kindersley, 1991.

Schlein, Miriam. *Let's Go Dinosaur Tracking!* New York: Harper Collins, 1991.

Simon, Seymour. *New Questions and Answers about Dinosaurs.* New York: Morrow Junior Books, 1990.

INDEX